World Book, Inc.
180 North LaSalle Street
Suite 900
Chicago, Illinois 60601
USA

For information about other "True or False?" titles, as well as other World Book print and digital publications, please go to www.worldbook.com.

For information about other World Book publications, call 1-800-WORLDBK (967-5325).

For information about sales to schools and libraries, call 1-800-975-3250 (United States) or 1-800-837-5365 (Canada).

Library of Congress Cataloging-in-Publication Data for this volume has been applied for.

True or False?
ISBN: 978-0-7166-3725-7 (set, hc.)

Planet Earth
ISBN: 978-0-7166-3732-5 (hc.)

Also available as:
ISBN: 978-0-7166-3742-4 (e-book)

Printed in China by Shenzhen Wing King Tong Paper Products Co., Ltd., Shenzhen, Guangdong
1st printing July 2018

Staff

Executive Committee

President
Jim O'Rourke

Vice President and
Editor in Chief
Paul A. Kobasa

Vice President, Finance
Donald D. Keller

Vice President, Marketing
Jean Lin

Vice President, International
Maksim Rutenberg

Vice President, Technology
Jason Dole

Director, Human Resources
Bev Ecker

Editorial

Director, New Print
Tom Evans

Writers
Grace Guibert
Mellonee Carrigan

Editor
Will Adams

Librarian
S. Thomas Richardson

Manager, Contracts and
Compliance
(Rights and Permissions)
Loranne K. Shields

Manager, Indexing Services
David Pofelski

Digital

Director, Digital Product
Development
Erika Meller

Digital Product Manager
Jonathan Wills

Manufacturing/Production

Manufacturing Manager
Anne Fritzinger

Production Specialist
Curley Hunter

Proofreader
Nathalie Strassheim

Graphics and Design

Senior Art Director
Tom Evans

Senior Visual
Communications Designer
Melanie Bender

Senior Designer
Isaiah Sheppard

Media Editor
Rosalia Bledsoe

TRUE OR FALSE?

PLANET EARTH

WORLD BOOK

www.worldbook.com

TRUE OR FALSE?

Earth is the third planet
from the sun.

TRUE!

Animals and plants can live almost
everywhere on Earth's surface
because it is just the right distance
from the sun. Living things need
the sun's warmth and light.

But if Earth were closer to the sun, it would be too hot for living things. If Earth were farther from the sun, it would be too cold.

JUPITER

MARS

EARTH

VENUS

MERCURY

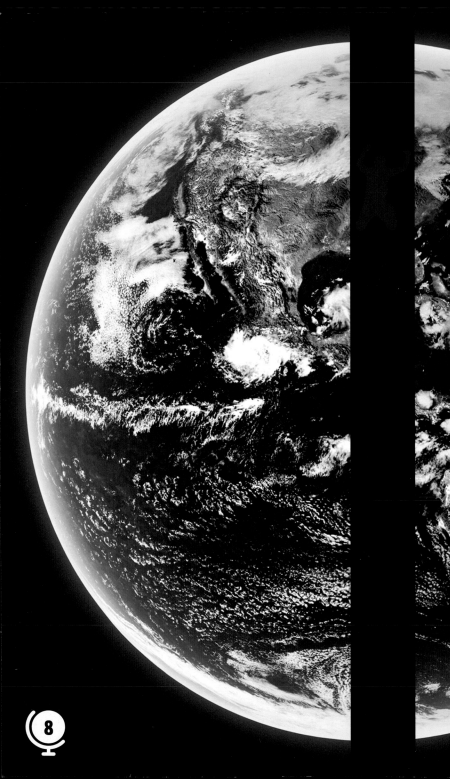

You can dig straight through Earth
and end up on the other side.

9

There are many reasons that people can't dig through Earth. That would be almost 8,000 miles (13,000 kilometers) of digging! The center of the Earth is much too hot for us to survive. It's 10,800 °F (6000 °C)—that's as hot as the surface of the sun!

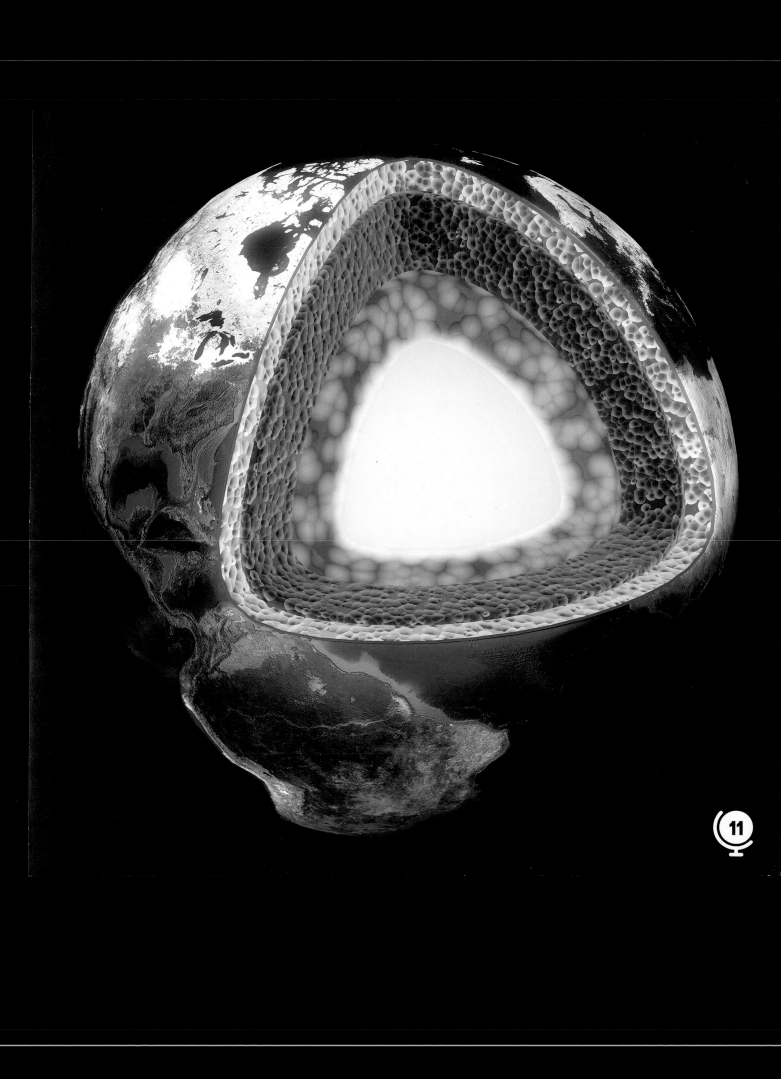

Earth is perfectly round in shape.

Earth appears to be round in pictures from space. But the planet bulges slightly at its middle as it spins around.

Earth is also slightly flat at the North and South poles. The difference is really too tiny to be seen.

Earth's surface is always changing.

TRUE!

Some of these changes happen suddenly. Earthquakes, volcanoes, and flash floods break, bury, and wash away pieces of Earth's surface. Other changes happen slowly.

Water and wind wear away rock over thousands or millions of years. For example, flowing water carved the Grand Canyon in North America out of hard rock.

The outer layer of Earth is called the Pizza Crust.

20

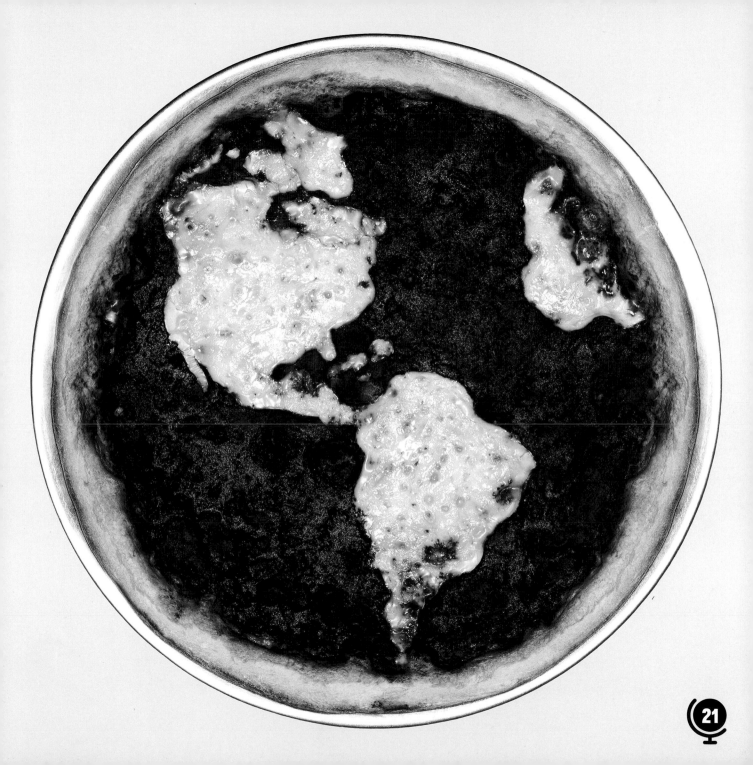

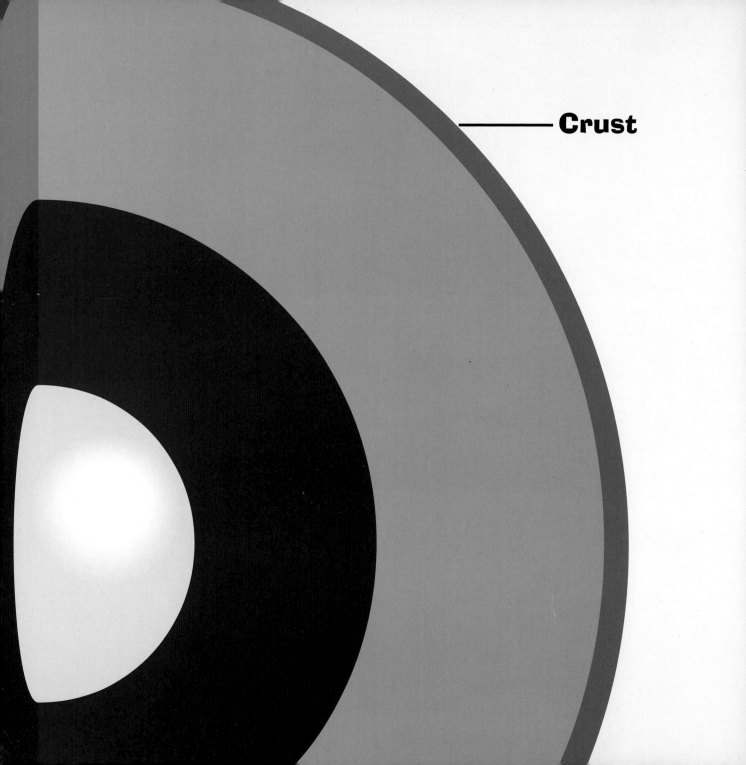

Crust

Underneath Earth's crust is solid rock.

It's just called the crust. The crust is the rocky "skin" that covers Earth. It is about 5 miles (8 kilometers) thick under the oceans and 25 miles (40 kilometers) thick under the continents.

TRUE OR FALSE?

The crust is made up of pieces like a puzzle.

Underneath the crust, Earth has three layers of rock and metal. These layers are the mantle, the outer core, and the inner core. The mantle is a layer of hot, melted rock below the crust. The outer core lies beneath the mantle. It is made mostly of melted iron, and is even hotter than the mantle!

The inner core is the hottest part of Earth. Scientists think the inner core is a ball of solid iron.

Land covers more than half
of Earth's surface.

Water covers about 70 percent of Earth's surface. Most of this water is in the oceans.

TRUE OR FALSE?

There are ten continents — the largest land masses.

North
America

FALSE!

South
America

There are usually said to be seven continents:
Asia, Africa, North America, South America,
Antarctica, Europe, and Australia. Technically,
Europe is not a continent, but a part of Asia.

Europe

Asia

Africa

Australia

Other people consider North and South America to be a single continent. One thing's certain: there are definitely less than ten!

Antarctica

There once was just one huge continent on Earth.

41

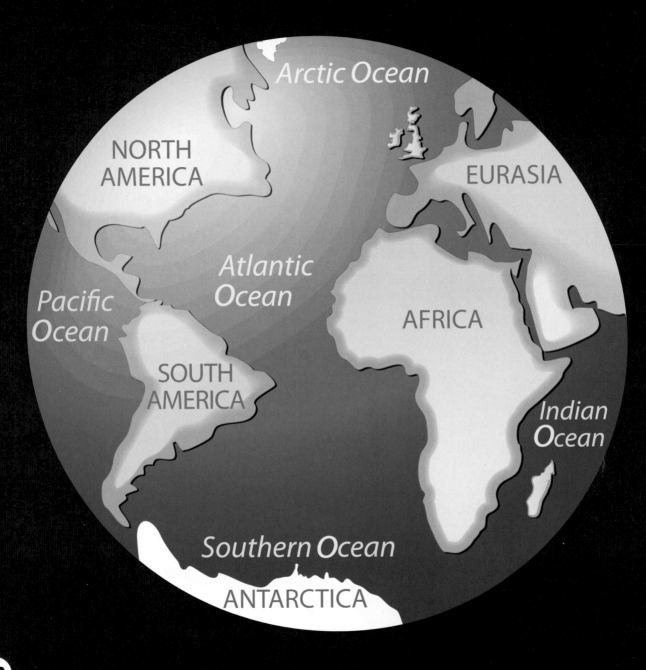

Hundreds of millions of years ago there was only one huge continent. Then it split into two large continents, which later broke apart, and the different landforms drifted away. The shifting plates moved Earth's continents to where they are today.

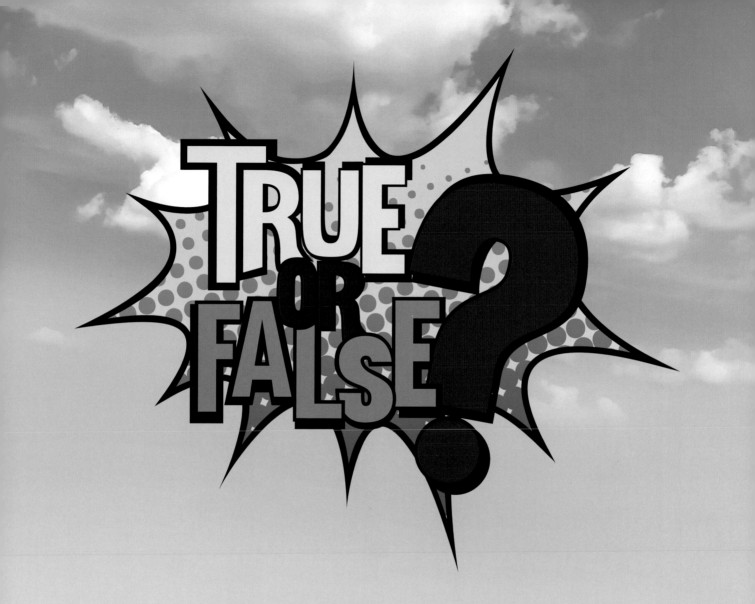

The oxygen we breathe comes from plants.

TRUE!

Plants aren't just pretty to look at. We need them to live! Plant cells make oxygen in the process of photosynthesis *(foh toh SIHN thuh sihs)*. Plant cells make their fuel from sunlight using photosynthesis, and they release oxygen into the air.

Scientists think that all the air's oxygen has been made by photosynthesis over billions of years. Nearly all living things need oxygen to stay alive!

Lightning only happens during thunderstorms.

There are many different types of lightning. Lightning is caused by energy in the air. Most of the time, we see lightning come from storm clouds. But there are many different causes. Lightning can even come from the clouds caused by an erupting volcano!

TRUE OR FALSE?

More than 2 million different kinds of bugs live in the Amazon rain forest.

TRUE!

The Amazon rain forest is home to a wider variety of plants and animals than any other place in the world. There are about 3,000 types of fish in its rivers.

More than 1,300 kinds of birds live in its trees. Tens of thousands of different types of plants grow in the Amazon rain forest.

Rain comes from holes in the sky.

Rain falls from clouds. Water on Earth rises into the air from lakes, rivers, and oceans in the form of water vapor. Water vapor is a gas form of water. Water vapor comes together in clouds. When the cloud cannot hold any more water, heavy drops fall to the ground as rain.

Most of Earth's water is undrinkable.

The oceans contain almost all of the water on Earth. This water is too salty to drink. Only about 3 percent of the world's water is fresh (not salty). Most of this water is not easy to get to because it's in the form of ice covering Antarctica, Greenland, and waters near the North Pole.

TRUE OR FALSE?

Areas with similar climate (weather patterns), plants, and animals are called biomes.

There are lots of different biomes that describe both land and sea habitats. Some biomes are the rain forest, the desert, the tundra, fresh water, and the ocean. A single type of biome can occur in many parts of the world. For example, the grassland biome in Asia is much like the grassland biome in North America!

TRUE OR FALSE?

All deserts are hot.

FALSE!

A desert is a region with very little rainfall. Most deserts are very hot, but some are very cold.

Deserts near the North and South poles are so cold that water freezes year round and plants can't grow there. These are called cold deserts or polar deserts.

TRUE OR FALSE?

The world's highest waterfall is so tall that some of the water never hits the ground.

TRUE!

Angel Falls, a waterfall in the country of Venezuela, is the tallest waterfall in the world. Because of its height, much of its water evaporates (turns into water vapor) as it falls! Angel Falls is 3,212 feet (979 meters) in total height.

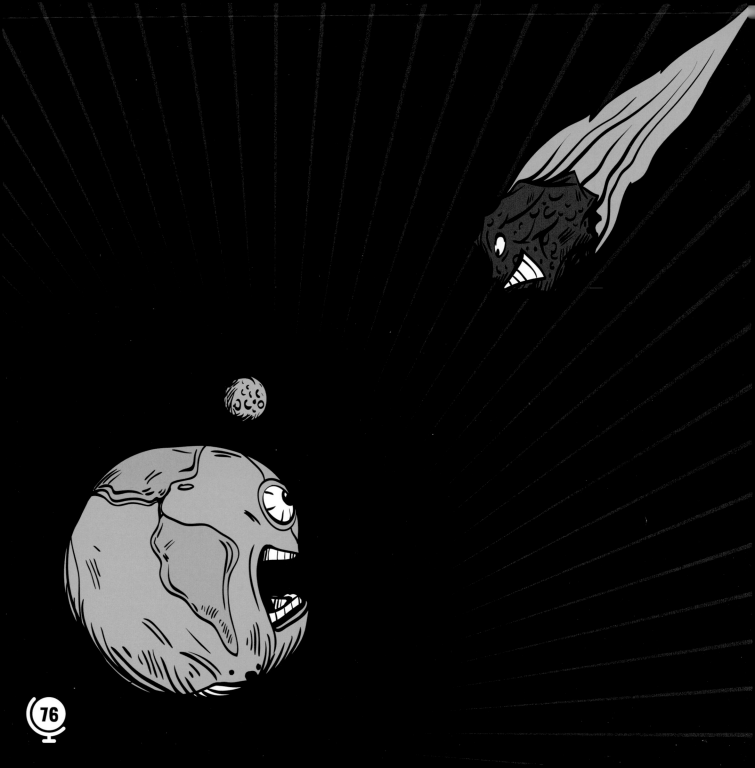

Earthquakes are caused by space rocks bumping into Earth.

77

Earthquakes happen when the plates of Earth's crust shift suddenly. Earthquakes are some of the most powerful events on Earth. They can damage buildings, bridges, and other structures. The strength of an earthquake depends on how much the Earth's plates shift.

Earth's climate is changing.

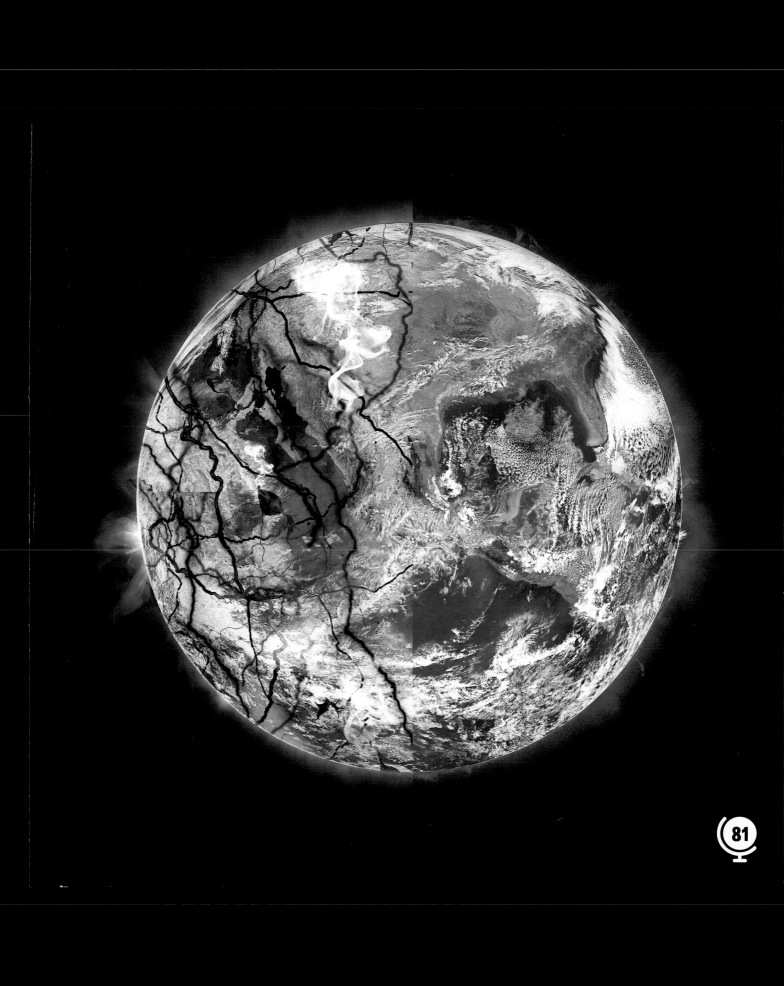

Earth has slowly grown warmer or cooler many times in the past. But in recent history, people have played a part in global warming, an increase in the average temperature at Earth's surface. Human activities have caused most of the warming since the mid-1900's. Scientists think that Earth's average surface temperature will rise even more by 2100.

83

TRUE OR FALSE?

Global warming can harm living things.

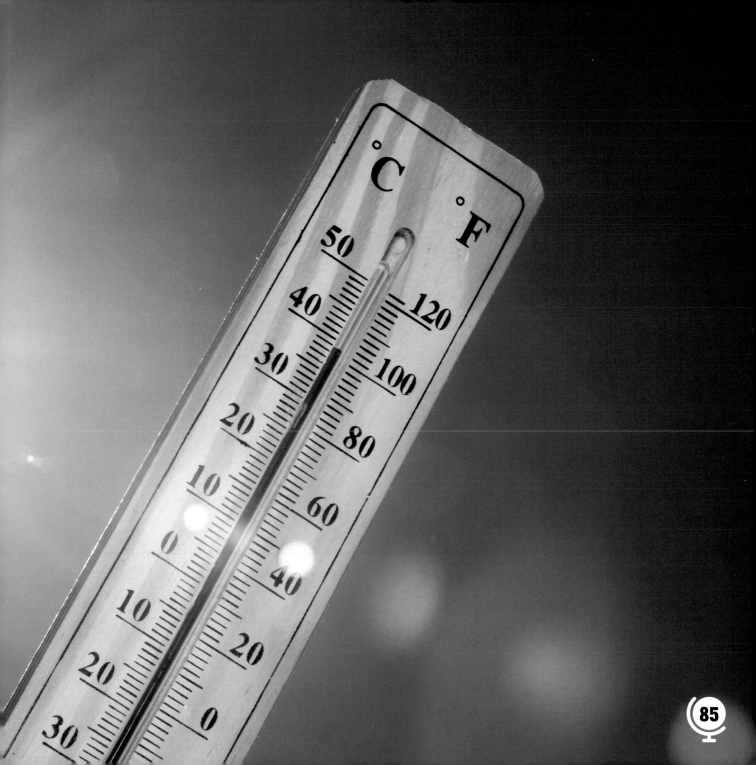

TRUE!

Even though it sounds like a warmer Earth would mean summer all the time, scientists warn that global warming will harm life. It can lead to more extreme weather, rising sea levels, destruction of animal habitats, and many other damaging effects.

There's nothing we can do
to stop global warming.

There are lots of ways to fight global warming. Many countries have agreed to work together to help. Lots of them are taking steps to cut the amount of harmful gasses entering the air from such things as cars and factories.

Some are using more energy from the sun or the wind to reduce the amount of fuels they burn. Every person can help limit global warming by turning off lights and electric appliances when not using them. It's important to take care of Earth!

DID YOU KNOW...

Lake Baikal in southeastern Russia is the **deepest lake** in the world.

Five million years ago, the Mediterranean Sea got cut off from the Atlantic Ocean, causing much of the sea **to dry up.**

The **lowest temperature** recorded on Earth was –129 °F (–89 °C) in Antarctica. **Brr!**

The air is mostly made up of a gas called **nitrogen.**

The
**highest
mountain,**
Mount Everest, is
29,035 feet (8,850
meters) high.

High up in the air, a
special kind of oxygen
called ozone reflects
some of the sun's
harmful rays.
This is called the
ozone layer.

Ozone layer

The equator
is an imaginary
circle that lies
halfway between the
North and
South poles.

Huge, **river-like currents**
flow through all of Earth's oceans.

Index

Acknowledgments

Cover: © Miumi/Shutterstock; © Aldo Murillo,
        iStockphoto; ©Ded Mazay, Shutterstock
4-19   © Shutterstock
21   © Butch Martin, Getty Images
22-93   © Shutterstock